From Blossom to Honey

From Blossom
to Honey

Ali Mitgutsch

 Carolrhoda Books, Inc., Minneapolis

First published in the United States of America 1981 by
Carolrhoda Books, Inc. All English language rights reserved.

Original edition © 1975 by Sellier Verlag GmbH, Eching bei München,
West Germany, under the title VON DER BLÜTE ZUM HONIG.
Revised English text © 1981 by Carolrhoda Books, Inc.
Illustrations © 1975 by Sellier Verlag GmbH.

Manufactured in the United States of America

LIBRARY OF CONGRESS CATALOGING IN PUBLICATION DATA

Mitgutsch, Ali.
From blossom to honey.

(A Carolrhoda start to finish book)
Edition for 1975 published under title: Von der Blüte
zum Honig.
SUMMARY: Describes how bees turn flower nectar
into the honey which the beekeeper extracts from the
hive.

1. Bee culture—Juvenile literature. 2. Honey—Juvenile literature. [1. Bee culture. 2. Honey] I. Title.

SF523.5.M5713 1981 638'.1 81-80
ISBN 0-87614-146-7

2 3 4 5 6 7 8 9 10 86 85 84 83 82

From Blossom
to Honey

When flowering plants blossom,
they produce a sweet liquid called **nectar** (NECK-ter).
The nectar is stored inside the flowers.
Bees use nectar to make honey.
They drink the nectar with their long tongues.
The nectar goes into the bee's honey stomach
where it mixes with chemicals from the bee's body.

When its honey stomach is full of nectar,
the bee flies back to its **hive**.
Some bees have natural hives
that they build themselves.
But when people want to collect honey,
they usually build hives for the bees.
There are six hives in this **beehouse**.
Each one is painted a different color.

Each bee knows which hive it lives in.
But just in case one makes a mistake,
one bee guards the entrance of each hive.

Wooden frames hang inside the beehives.
The bees have built wax **honeycomb**
in these frames.
The bees unload their nectar
in the cells of the honeycomb.
Then they seal each filled compartment
with a wax cap.
Inside the compartments,
the water evaporates from the nectar,
and it changes into honey.

Now the honey is ready to be collected
by the **beekeeper**.
The beekeeper must wear special clothing
so that the bees can't sting him.
He wears a long coat, a hat with a veil,
and gloves.

First the beekeeper takes the hives out of the beehouse.
Then he takes the wooden frames out of the hives.
While the beekeeper takes out the frames,
the bees buzz about excitedly.
But they can't sting him through his special clothing.

Now the beekeeper puts the frames into a machine
called a honey **extractor** (ehk-STRAKT-er).
He cuts the wax caps off the honeycomb with a hot knife.
When he turns the handle,
the frames whirl around very fast.
Soon all the honey drains out of the honeycomb.
The beekeeper puts the honey into air-tight containers
so it will stay fresh for a long time.
Then he takes the remaining honeycomb off the frames
and puts the frames back into the beehives.
The bees will soon build more honeycomb on the frames.

Now the honey is ready to be eaten.

Honey makes many things sweet and delicious.

It is good even when it is eaten all by itself!

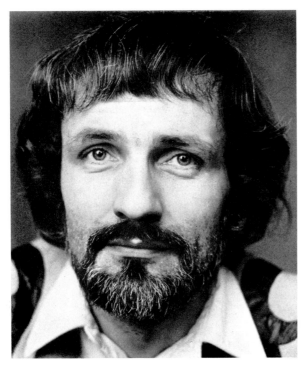

Ali
Mitgutsch

ALI MITGUTSCH is one of Germany's best-known
children's book illustrators. He is a devoted world traveler, and
many of his book ideas have taken shape during his travels.
Perhaps this is why they have such international appeal.
Mr. Mitgutsch's books have been published in 22 countries
and are enjoyed by thousands of readers around the world.

Ali Mitgutsch lives with his wife and three children in
Schwabing, the artists' quarter in Munich. The Mitgutsch
family also enjoys spending time on their farm in the Bavarian
countryside.

THE CAROLRHODA

 START

From Beet to Sugar

From Blossom to Honey

From Cacao Bean to Chocolate

From Cement to Bridge

From Clay to Bricks

From Cotton to Pants

From Cow to Shoe

From Dinosaurs to Fossils

From Egg to Bird

From Egg to Butterfly

From Fruit to Jam

From Grain to Bread

From Grass to Butter

From Ice to Rain

From Milk to Ice Cream

From Oil to Gasoline

From Ore to Spoon

From Sand to Glass

From Seed to Pear

From Sheep to Scarf

From Tree to Table

 TO FINISH

BOOKS